Calshot Cas

HAMPSHIRE

J G COAD MA, FSA
Inspector of Ancient Monuments

Calshot Castle was built in 1539-40 to guard the entrance to Southampton Water. It formed part of the chain of coastal defences built by Henry VIII to counter possible invasion following his break with the Roman Catholic Church. The castle's fortunes have fluctuated, reflecting national concern with defence.

Substantial repairs and alterations were made in 1584, again in the 1770s during the American War of Independence, during the Napoleonic Wars and at the beginning of the twentieth century. In 1913 Calshot became one of the first Royal Navy seaplane bases. It was manned during both world wars, and between the wars was well known for its links with the Schneider Trophy air races.

The castle still retains most of its 1540 work and appearance, despite its later alterations and uses, and demonstrates how the problem of protecting the Solent from enemy ships was tackled over a period of nearly 400 years. This guidebook contains a tour of the castle and relates its fascinating history.

CONTENTS

3   TOUR OF THE CASTLE
5   Keep exterior
5   Keep interior
5   *First floor*
6   *Second floor*
6   *Roof*
7   *Keep basement*
8   Courtyard
9   Gatehouse

10   HISTORY
10   The Tudor castle
10   *The threat to England*
11   *Defence of the Solent*
12   Calshot in the seventeenth and eighteenth centuries
14   Garrison life
17   The coastguards
18   The re-arming of the 1890s
20   Calshot Royal Naval Air Station
22   Twentieth-century Calshot

25   GLOSSARY
25   BIBLIOGRAPHY
25   DOCUMENTARY SOURCES

PLANS
4   Plan of Calshot Castle
7   Cross-section of Calshot Castle
13   Defences of the Solent
23   Late nineteenth- and twentieth-century defences of Southampton Water

Visit our website at www.english-heritage.org.uk
Published by English Heritage
23 Saville Row, London W1S 2ET
© Copyright English Heritage 1991
First Published 1986
Second edition 1991, reprinted 1994, 1996, 2005
Printed in England by The Colourhouse
Dd 6073917, 04/05, C10, 0563, 38776, 04908
ISBN 1 85074 102 6

TOUR OF THE CASTLE

Calshot from the southeast, showing the three-storeyed keep encircled by the curtain wall, with the rear of the gatehouse on the left and the coastguard tower on the right

Calshot, like all of Henry VIII's coastal fortresses, is notable for its precise, symmetrical planning and the quality of its masonry. Dominating the castle is the central three-storey gun-tower or keep, made more conspicuous since the lowering of the surrounding curtain wall in the eighteenth century. Facing the landward approach is the gatehouse, now reached by a fixed metal-framed bridge, installed in the nineteenth century. The original bridge could be raised as an additional safeguard (see illustration, page 16). The stone-lined moat, although shallow, presented a further and formidable obstacle to attackers who would have been under fire from heavy weapons and hand guns from whatever angle they chose to assault the castle.

Since its completion in 1540 the castle has undergone quite substantial modifications, although its basic form and outline would still be instantly recognisable to Henry VIII and his military engineers and masons.

In common with all other castles and fortresses, the design of Calshot is a balance between the need to make the castle as powerful as possible and the requirements of its garrison for living quarters and space for stores. Until its extension in the 1770s the gatehouse accommodation was very limited, so the bulk of the living space was within the keep. This would have been where the master gunner, his family and other members of the garrison lived, sharing the second floor with the heavy weapons mounted there. Not surprisingly, there is evidence that from time to time members of the garrison preferred accommodation in small houses built nearby on the spit.

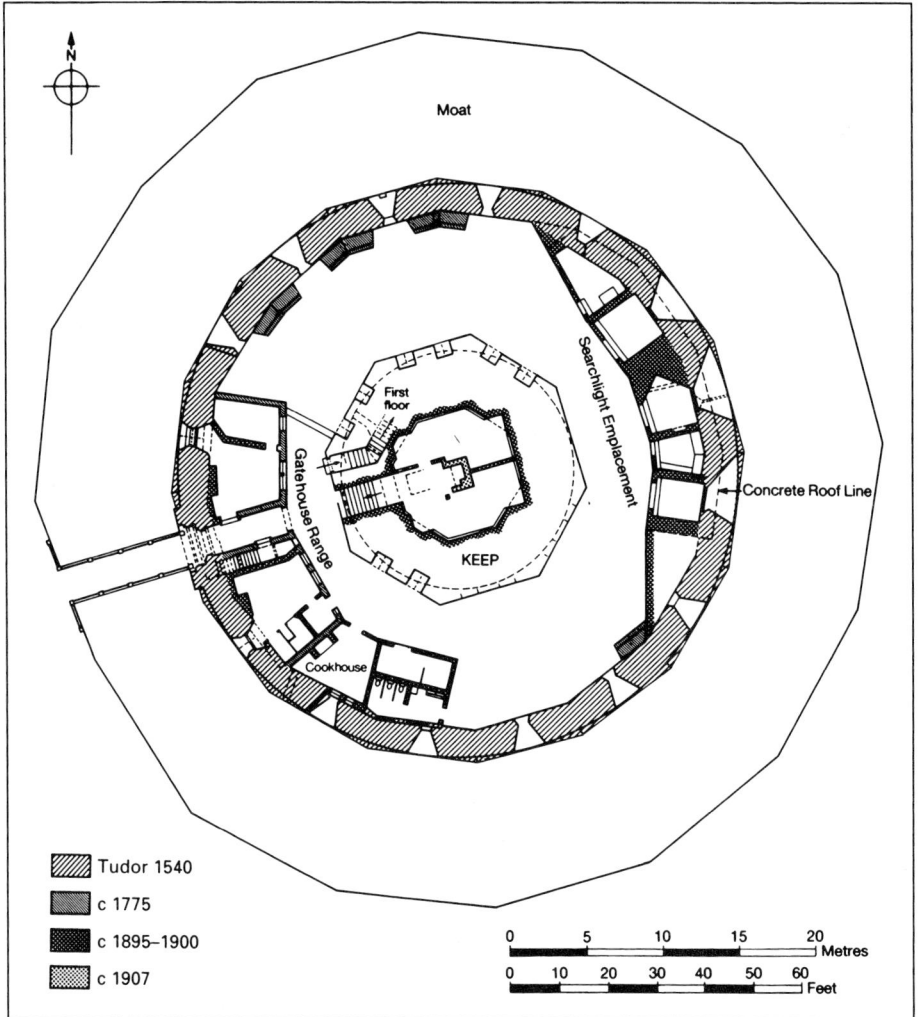

N

Moat

First floor

Searchlight Emplacement

Concrete Roof Line

Gatehouse Range

KEEP

Cookhouse

Tudor 1540

c 1775

c 1895–1900

c 1907

0	5	10	15	20
				Metres

0	10	20	30	40	50	60
						Feet

Plan of the ground floor or Calshot Castle

Visitors to the castle may like to view the exterior of the keep before looking at the rooms inside and climbing to the roof to enjoy the magnificent views. It is suggested that you then return to the courtyard and see the keep basement and searchlight emplacements before returning to the gatehouse. The following description of the castle broadly follows this sequence; a cross section of the castle is on page 7.

Keep exterior

Externally, the least-altered part of the castle is the central gun-tower of keep. This has an octagonal lower storey, imitating the shape of the outer curtain and moat, but the upper two floors, although octagonal in plan inside, present a cylindrical exterior to the world. Only the top has been substantially modified, first in the eighteenth century when its curved parapets with their embrasures (openings) for heavy guns (see illustration, page 15) were replaced by the existing unbroken parapet designed to shield soldiers using hand weapons. In its turn, this parapet was further modified on the southeastern side in 1907 by the addition of mass concrete to form emplacements for two 12 pounder (pdr) guns (12 lb represents the weight of the shot fired) ordered to be mounted on the roof.

At ground level, the exterior of the keep is provided with recesses, some now blocked, which probably once housed powder and shot for the courtyard guns. The wooden sliding door opposite the gatehouse leads to an access to the basement formed as part of the modification here in the 1890s. Before then, the only entrance to the keep was the small doorway to the left. High above this are the remains of a metal bracket which once carried the castle bell. The carved royal shield above the sliding door has

been reset here; its original location is not known.

Keep interior

Go through the small doorway and up the stairs from the courtyard to the first floor. The stairs were extensively re-formed and their line altered as part of the modifications begun in 1896. This was to allow the insertion at a different and slightly higher level of a very strong concrete ceiling over the basement to protect the engines and generators then being installed there (see page 18). As a safety precaution, the original access to the basement from a doorway leading from the first flight of stairs was sealed. The blocking is clearly visible about half way up.

First floor

The first floor, although retaining its sixteenth-century outline, looks much as it did when converted to a barrack room for eleven men at the end of the nineteenth century (see page 24). The match-board lining to the walls dates from this phase, but above this is the Tudor stonework, much of it is still reddened from the fire which gutted the keep in the early 1580s. The floor here and in the passage outside was lowered some 2 feet during the alterations of the 1890s, taking advantage of space gained during work to the basement (see page 7) – hence the high window sills in this room. In the passage can be seen the blocked top of the arch over the stairway which once led to the basement.

The barrack stove, a modern replacement, is linked into the original Tudor flue; below this are the remains of the sixteenth-century fireplace, the base of its right-hand jamb or side pillar indicative of the original floor level here. The fireplace can be seen by opening the panelling at this point.

In the floor and ceiling the rectangular outlines in the centre of the room mark the site of the ammunition hoist inserted from the basement to the roof in 1907 (see page 20).

Second floor

The top floor of the keep has similarly been considerably altered, although its walls are largely Tudor. Along with the roof, this level once carried heavy guns, perhaps some of the culverins or demi-culverins (cannon) known to have been here in 1623. These would have been fired through the large embrasures. This room was also used as garrison accommodation and may very well have been partitioned into smaller areas. In the southeast side is a small garderobe or latrine fitted into the thickness of the wall, while in other bays can be seen the blocked remains of two Tudor fireplaces. The present windows are nineteenth-century replacements of earlier ones; the Tudor garrison may have had to make do with wooden shutters.

The sixteenth-century masonry on this floor has been extensively damaged. Much of it was replaced by concrete and brick during the late Victorian alterations into a barrack room for fourteen men. The timber lining to the walls installed as part of these modifications has long gone. The massive girders carrying the roof are comparatively modern, replacing ones installed here in 1907 to help support the new battery above.

Roof

The stairs continue to roof level, now dominated by the massive concrete mounts for the two 12pdr guns. In the bases, metal doors protect ready-use ammunition lockers. The lockers on the left both held 180 shells; those on the right contained 80 cartridges with a further 40

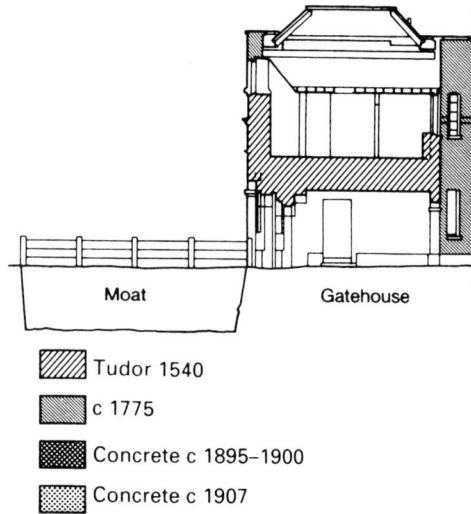

Moat   Gatehouse

Tudor 1540

c 1775

Concrete c 1895–1900

Concrete c 1907

in the recess between the steps to the guns. The ammunition hoist associated with these once terminated in the centre of the roof. This has long been removed and the outline in the asphalt marks the site of brick and concrete buildings last used by the coastguard service.

A 12pdr quick-firing (QF) gun is displayed on one of the gun positions. This is the same type as those installed here in 1907, but its shield and mounting are different as it was formerly fitted on a warship.

The parapet probably dates from the alterations of the 1770s and it is likely that at this time the roof was re-formed to a shallow conical shape covered in lead. This allowed for a narrow walkway for soldiers immediately behind the parapet. This arrangement survived substantially intact until the present flat concrete roof was installed in 1907.

On a fine day there are spectacular views up Southampton Water past Fawley

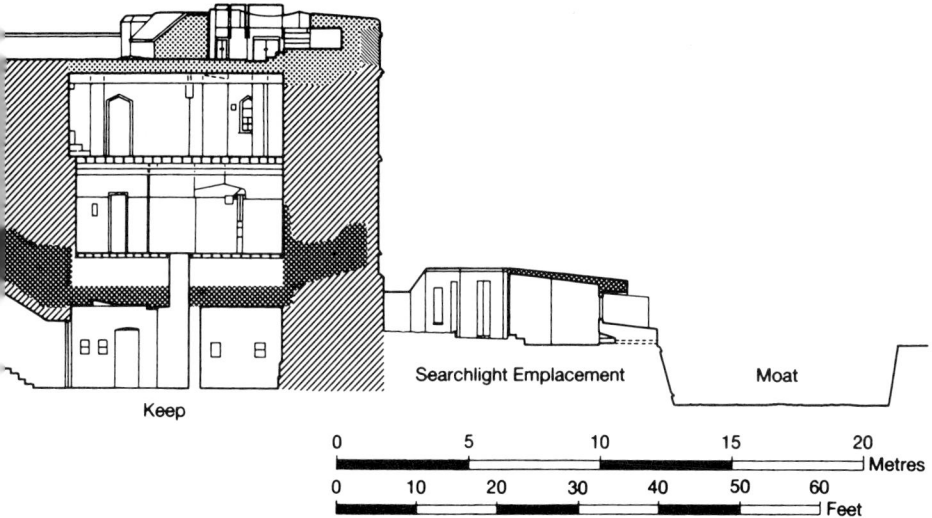

Searchlight Emplacement   Moat

Keep

```
0          5          10         15         20
                                              Metres
0    10    20    30    40    50    60
                                      Feet
```

Cross section through Calshot Castle

oil refinery and south to the Isle of Wight across the busy Solent. A little up Southampton Water on the far side are the oil storage tanks at Hamble; on the foreshore south of these stood St Andrew's Castle, while further along woods conceal the site of Netley Castle. Between these two a domed structure is all that remains of the Royal Victoria Hospital, a monster building some 1424 feet long built between 1856 and 1863 as the main military hospital in Great Britain. Well sited for the army's troop ships and hospital ships, its use declined as the British Empire waned and aircraft replaced ships; most of it was demolished in 1966.

Keep basement

The original form of the Tudor basement is mostly unknown, so thorough were the alterations here between 1896 and 1907. It is probable that it was vaulted as at Hurst Castle, built by the same team after they had completed Calshot in 1540.

The former existence of a vault there would account for the considerable space existing between the top of the present reinforced basement ceiling and the first-floor room above.

The original function of the basement was as a storeroom, not just for gunpowder and shot, but also for the provisions, fuel and equipment needed by the garrison. There were probably water tanks or casks too, for it seems likely that any well sunk on this end of the site would at best have yielded only brackish water.

In 1896, when it had been decided that Calshot should have defence electric lights (searchlights), the basement was chosen to house the oil engines, generators and batteries. It was then that the existing entrance was formed and the basement lined with brick and possibly deepened. It seems very probable that this was when the vault, if it existed, was removed and replaced by the present heavy concrete ceiling.

In 1907 the engines and their equipment were removed to a new building outside the castle, making way for the conversion of the basement to a magazine for the new guns on the roof. The brick cross wall with its lamp niches and the remains of the ammunition hoist date from this work. Not all trace of its use as a generating room has been lost, however: outside on the northwest side of the keep are massive iron brackets and part of the exhaust pipes from the oil engines.

Courtyard

When completed in 1540 the sixteen-sided curtain wall around the courtyard with its beautifully flared apron sloping into the moat was considerably higher than now. The courtyard guns fired through fifteen embrasures - the gatehouse occupied the sixteenth side - while above the embrasures was a deep parapet shielding defenders armed with hand weapons on the wall walk behind. This arrangement, clearly visible in the illustration below, probably remained unaltered until the work in the 1770s. Perhaps to save maintenance, or possibly to give the gunners in the keep a better field of fire close to the castle, the curtain was then lowered to its present height and stone firing steps were built between the gun embrasures (see opposite). At the same time the gatehouse was extended in width, the extension preserving the original embrasures on either side of the entrance.

On the northeast side of the courtyard, overlooking the entrance to Southampton Water, the long concrete building against the inside of the curtain was constructed c1896 to house searchlights. These were used in conjunction with a new gun battery south of the castle (see aerial view on page 21) and with the boom defences across Southampton Water. The Tudor embrasures were cut back to enable

Calshot from the west, by F Armstrong. This early eighteenth-century view shows the Tudor curtain wall before it was reduced in height, removing the heads of the gun embrasures (From a private collection)

Guns in the courtyard covering Southampton Water. Note the firing steps between the gun embrasures

the searchlights to have a better arc. Two signalling lamps from HMS *Tiger* have been installed here to give an impression of the size of the original equipment.

Gatehouse

As first built, the gatehouse was a simple two-storey structure, probably with a single room over the gate passage. Above this, the roof had provision for guns, while the engraving by Armstrong opposite shows it flanked by a further gun embrasure at first-floor level on its western side.

From outside the castle the gatehouse presents a largely blank front to the world. The doors of the gate passage were once protected by a portcullis (defensive grill) operated from the room above; the grooves for the portcullis remain prominent. Above

the entrance the blank panel with its Renaissance pilasters probably held the coat-of-arms of Henry VIII; flanking this are two dumb-bell loops for hand-guns.

In the 1770s the gatehouse was enlarged to provide better accommodation for the governor. The building was heightened and widened, but in deference to its continuing military role, all windows except one were placed to overlook the courtyard. The accommodation thus provided has been extensively modernised internally.

Part of the 1896 alterations can be seen in the present arrangement of the guardroom with its cell on the western side of the gate passage. Contemporary with this are the brick buildings attached to the southern end of the gatehouse; the louvred room was the garrison cookhouse with storerooms and latrines beyond.

HISTORY

Henry VIII was responsible for building a
whole chain of fortresses along the coast to
protect against possible invasion. Portrait after
Holbein c1536 (National Portrait Gallery)

Pope Paul III, Alessandro Farnese, who
excommunicated King Henry in 1538
following the annulment of his marriage to
Catherine of Aragon

The Tudor castle

The threat to England

Calshot Castle, on the end of a short
shingle spit jutting into the entrance of
Southampton Water, was one fruit of the
political upheavals and uncertainties
surrounding England in the late 1530s
following Henry VIII's break with the
Roman Catholic Church, the annulment
of the King's marriage to Catherine of
Aragon, aunt of the Emperor Charles V,
and the decision by Pope Paul III in
December 1538 to order the
implementation of the Bull of
excommunication against Henry.

In itself, this Bull posed little threat to
the King, but its enactment six months
after the two principal Catholic monarchs
of Europe, Charles V and Francis I of
France, had signed a peace treaty raised
the possibility of an invasion of England in
the guise of a Catholic crusade.

Early in 1539, Henry began
preparations to resist such a threat. As
immediate counter-measures, musters of
able-bodied men were held, additional
weapons and mercenaries were sought in
Hamburg and Antwerp and the small royal
fleet was prepared. To alert these forces,
the warning chain of beacons around the
coast was repaired and manned.

Such arrangements could be made
comparatively quickly, but in themselves
their effectiveness against a well-organised
invasion force was questionable. More
significantly, as part of a longer-term

strategy, in February 1539 the King appointed special commissioners to survey the coasts of England to choose locations for defence works to protect vulnerable invasion points, dockyards, fleet anchorages, ports and harbours. The work of these commissioners was to result in a series of forts from Milford Haven in west Wales to Hull on the east coast. This chain was the first system of coastal defence since the Saxon Shore forts built by the Romans over 1,200 years before.

Defence of the Solent

The area of the Solent was of special concern. Towards its eastern end lay Portsmouth, the only naval base south of the Thames, which rose in importance with the development of a standing navy in the early sixteenth century. Up Southampton Water lay the rich mercantile port of Southampton, a major centre of overseas trade enjoying easy access to its hinterland. The Isle of Wight itself needed protection, for an enemy securely established there could control the Solent and be very difficult to dislodge.

William Fitzwilliam, the Lord Admiral and Earl of Southampton, and William Paulet, Lord St John, were the two commissioners charged with the responsibility for devising a scheme of fortifications to protect this area. They recommended four forts: at Calshot, East and West Cowes, flanking the River Medina, and on the end of the shingle spit at Hurst overlooking the Needles Passage. The immediate surroundings of Portsmouth were to be protected by a separate series of defence works.

On Tuesday 18 March 1539 the two commissioners inspected Calshot Point from ships' boats and selected the exact location for the new castle. Calshot Spit was well positioned to dominate the shipping route to Southampton, for the deep-water channel runs close to the shore here. Construction of the two island forts and Calshot began almost immediately – 170 men were at work on East Cowes by April, an indication of the urgency of the situation - but the fear of invasion was so great that temporary earth and timber gun batteries were also erected near the Cowes forts as well as at Hurst and possibly at Calshot pending completion of the stone fortifications.

Calshot Castle was largely finished by the end of 1540 when the building team shifted to Hurst. On the latter's completion in early 1544, two more fortifications were built further up Southampton Water. St Andrew's Castle (c1543/4) was sited on the foreshore guarding the entrance to the river Hamble. Mid-way between this and Southampton, which still enjoyed a measure of protection behind its increasingly obsolete and vulnerable medieval walls. William Paulet sited Netley Castle (c1544) on his own land.

These castles were not only part of a systematic and well-planned defence scheme. They also marked a radical break, for they were the first fortifications in England to be specifically designed to mount artillery (cannon) and to resist the battering of enemy guns. Characteristic features are the round central tower, tiers of gun positions, immensely thick walls and curved parapets, the last designed to deflect enemy shot. The larger castles such as Hurst, and Deal in Kent, were provided with semi-circular bastions arranged symmetrically around their circumference.

These squat, powerful forts, difficult to hit from a moving ship, stood in marked contrast to their medieval predecessors with their high walls, now vulnerable to the power of the new ordnance (artillery). Henry VIII himself took a close interest in the design, which owed much to contemporary work in what is now southern Germany. Although the Italian type of pointed angle bastion was to supersede the rounded German pattern before the end of the 1540s, many of Henry's fortresses had active lives well into the twentieth century. Their design, although vulnerable to prolonged siege warfare, was quite strong enough in the context of bombardment from a ship, for which they had been primarily designed.

Calshot was one of the smaller fortresses, consisting of the three-storey central tower or keep surrounded by a lower concentric curtain wall and stone-lined moat. Within this comparatively small envelope, it mounted an armament perfectly adequate to its task of commanding the entrance to Southampton Water. Its eight embrasures and eighteen gun-ports were in three main tiers: in the curtain wall, on the second floor of the keep and on the keep roof. The gatehouse roof had space for three guns in case an attack was expected along the spit, while it is possible that guns were also mounted on the first floor of the keep.

There are few surviving details relating to the actual building of Calshot Castle but the accounts indicate that the major construction work was done in 1539 and 1540. Very probably much of the building stone came from one of the nearby abbeys such as Netley or Beaulieu, then in the course of demolition and adaptation after the Dissolution of the Monasteries. Certainly the lead for the roof came from Beaulieu Abbey, Henry VIII himself signing the warrant for its use in the autumn of 1539. A few months later in the early part of 1540 a garrison was established at the castle in the charge of a captain. He was assisted by a deputy and controlled eight gunners and five soldiers.

The invasion scare which had prompted the building of Calshot and its sister fortresses had largely passed before the chain of defences was completed. For the next 200 years or so its history is uneventful and obscure but the few references to Calshot indicate that it continued to be regarded as important by government. Some sort of garrison seems to have been maintained and the fabric of the castle was kept in reasonable repair. At the end of the 1540s it was one of the most heavily armed of the Solent fortresses, with a total of 36 guns, but by 1559 the number of serviceable weapons had fallen to ten. In 1584 Queen Elizabeth's government devoted funds to the repair of several of the Solent defences as part of its precautions against a possible Spanish invasion from Spain or the Netherlands. Calshot itself had suffered a serious fire which had gutted the keep – the reddening or calcining of the stonework which is still visible inside is a witness to this conflagration - and repairs needed 127 trees from the New Forest. Its garrison in the early 1580s numbered one master gunner and seven gunners.

Calshot in the seventeenth and eighteenth centuries

The civil war in the middle of the seventeenth century saw the end of Calshot's nearest neighbours when both Netley and St Andrew's Castles were disabled by Parliamentary forces at the end of 1642. Calshot probably owes its survival to an appreciation by Parliament of the continuing need to guard the entrance to Southampton Water. This need was never more acute than during the various wars of the eighteenth and early nineteenth centuries when each conflict engendered either invasion scares or fears of raids by enemy warships or privateers.

During the War of Spanish Succession (1702-13), Calshot was equipped with a maximum of twenty-five guns; by 1725

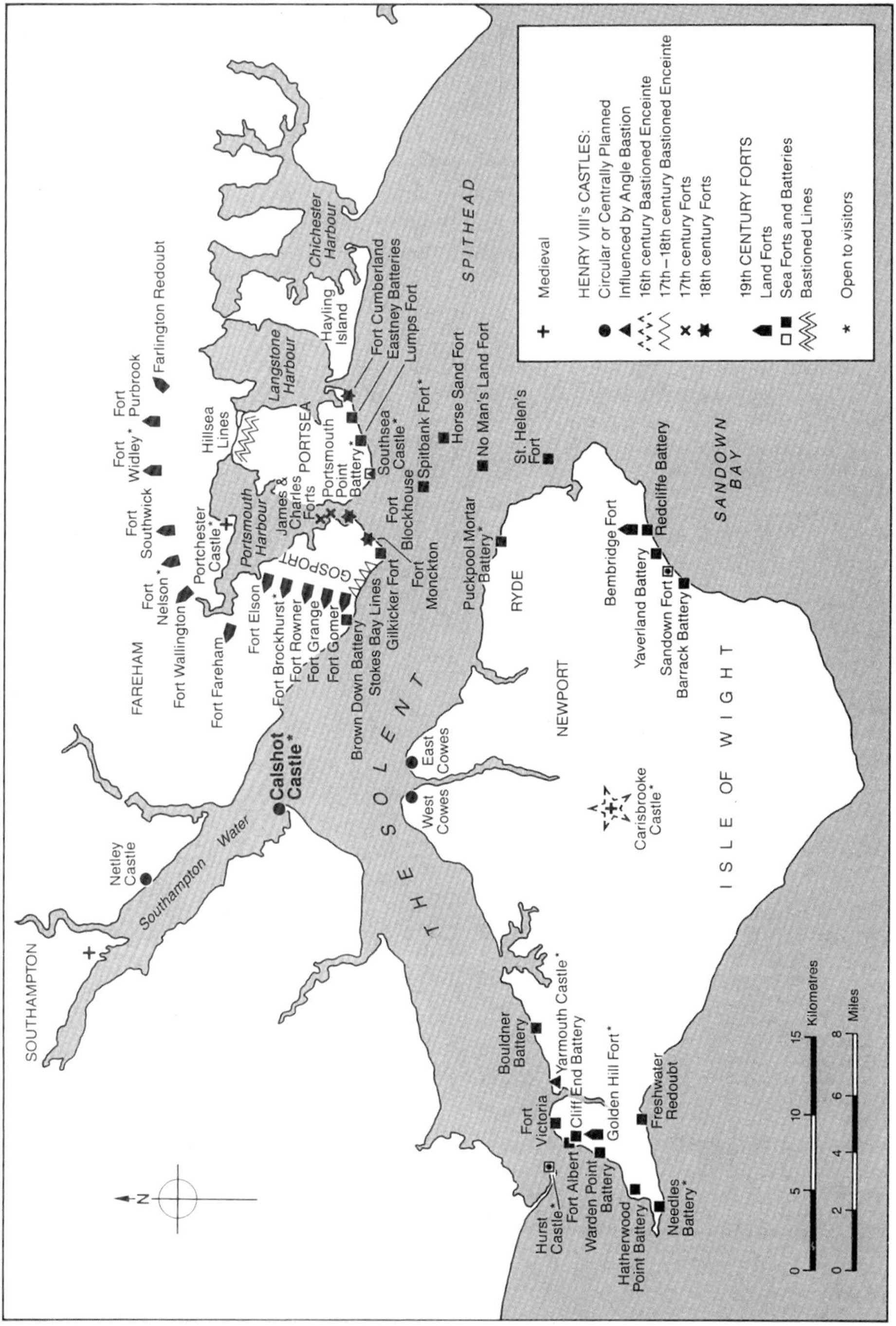
SOUTHAMPTON
Netley Castle
Southampton Water
Calshot Castle*
FAREHAM
Fort Wallington
Fort Nelson*
Fort Southwick
Fort Widley*
Fort Purbrook
Farlington Redoubt
Fort Fareham
Portchester Castle*
Portsmouth Harbour
Hillsea Lines
Langstone Harbour
Hayling Island
Chichester Harbour
Fort Elson
Fort Brockhurst*
Fort Rowner
Fort Grange
Fort Gomer
GOSPORT
James & Charles Forts
PORTSEA
Portsmouth Point Battery*
Southsea Castle*
Fort Cumberland
Eastney Batteries
Lumps Fort
Brown Down Battery
Stokes Bay Lines
Gilkicker Fort
Fort Monckton
Fort Blockhouse
Spitbank Fort*
Horse Sand Fort
No Man's Land Fort
SPITHEAD
THE SOLENT
East Cowes
West Cowes
Puckpool Mortar Battery*
RYDE
St. Helen's Fort
NEWPORT
Carisbrooke Castle*
Bembridge Fort
Redcliffe Battery
Yaverland Battery
Sandown Fort
Barrack Battery
SANDOWN BAY
ISLE OF WIGHT
Bouldner Battery
Yarmouth Castle*
Cliff End Battery
Golden Hill Fort*
Fort Victoria
Fort Albert
Hurst Castle*
Warden Point Battery
Hatherwood Point Battery
Freshwater Redoubt
Needles Battery*
N
Medieval
HENRY VIII's CASTLES:
Circular or Centrally Planned
Influenced by Angle Bastion
16th century Bastioned Enceinte
17th–18th century Bastioned Enceinte
17th century Forts
18th century Forts
19th CENTURY FORTS
Land Forts
Sea Forts and Batteries
Bastioned Lines
Open to visitors
0 5 10 15 Kilometres
0 2 4 6 8 Miles

A simplified map of the defences of the Solent area

this number had fallen to thirteen 6-pounders (guns were defined by the weight of their shot) in the charge of a master gunner and two gunners. In the wars at the end of the eighteenth century the armament fluctuated around a figure of nine 18-pounders and four 6-pounders. These, however, were not always fit to be used; in the 1780s and 1790s there were several complaints about the 'very old and defective' guns, while the wooden gun carriages were often found to be rotten. However, such defects had probably been overcome by the beginning of the long years of war with France (1793-1802; 1803-15).

The first significant alteration to the fabric of the Tudor castle did not take place until 1774. Then, as part of a programme of general repairs, the gatehouse was altered to much of its present appearance by the addition of a new set of rooms on the first floor for the governor or captain of the castle. By September 1777, 'the new rooms built for the use of the governor . . . have been wainscoted, the windows, tiling and fireplace of different buildings repaired'. The road to Fawley had also been improved, but much work remained to be done: the drawbridge was reported to be in a 'miserable condition'.

It is possible that this repair campaign of the mid-1770s also lowered the curtain wall, turning the gun-ports there into the present embrasured openings. The view engraved by the Buck brothers (right) clearly shows the original arrangement which may have given better protection to the gunners. After these alterations, it was to be over a century before further major structural works took place at the castle.

Garrison life

Garrison life at Calshot, although some way from the nearest settlement, was not as isolated as that at Hurst Castle. There are very few references to the men who lived here and it must be presumed that the manning of Calshot followed the arrangements common to other coastal forts. The pattern established in the sixteenth century was to be broadly followed until the abolition of coastal artillery in 1956. In peacetime, the permanent garrison usually numbered a few gunners in the charge of the master gunner. These men were responsible for keeping the armament in reasonable order, seeing that stores were adequate and generally looking after the castle. Peacetime government indifference and shortage of money meant that these objectives were seldom realised even well into the nineteenth century, as numerous reports bear witness. The outbreak of war was usually followed by a flurry of activity

Calshot from the south in 1773. This view by the Buck brothers shows the Tudor castle little altered since its completion

to remedy defects due to years of neglect.

Postings to these coastal forts, which seldom involved any arduous work, tended to be awarded to men who had served with the artillery trains and who were less fit to continue to serve in the field as a result of wounds or age. In effect permanent fortress garrisons were a convenient way of providing a kind of pension to those fortunate enough to secure a position in them. One consequence, common well into the nineteenth century, was that men and their families tended to remain in one fortress for years, many men very often dying in post.

Such caretaker garrisons were of course far too small to be able to man all the guns in wartime. In Tudor England, the government looked to the local militia or possibly even to mercenaries hired abroad to augment numbers. Such comparatively

ad hoc arrangements persisted well into the eighteenth century when the outbreak of war saw permanent garrisons supplemented by 'extraordinary or additional gunners' from naval seamen, infantry garrisons, county militias or even local inhabitants. Occasionally, men from the Royal Artillery would be sent to help.

In 1771 an attempt was made to regularise this system when eight 'Invalid Companies' were formed within the Royal Artillery. These new companies absorbed all the men in coastal fortress garrisons as well as others no longer fit enough for the field artillery. This permanent nucleus of trained personnel was to be supplemented in wartime by the raising, often through local initiative, of volunteer companies. This arrangement did not work to the best advantage of coastal artillery, for service in the latter tended to be treated by officers and men as very much second best to serving with the Royal Artillery proper. It was not, however, to be remedied until June 1899 when the Royal Garrison Artillery was formed and was able to develop its own separate identity, career structure and *esprit de corps*.

Initially, each coastal fortress was in the charge of a captain who would normally hold office only during hostilities. Charles I abolished this title and replaced it with that of governor, an office frequently awarded to men with little or no military experience; a lieutenant-governor, always a military officer, or, in less important fortresses such as Calshot, the master gunner did the actual work.

Little is known about the captains and governors of Calshot, but perhaps the most notable was Sir Henry Burrard (1755-1813). He came from a local family and was probably appointed in 1780, the year he became MP for Lymington after seeing service in North America under Sir William Howe. Burrard was to have an active if undistinguished military career in North America, Flanders, on the Copenhagen expedition in 1807 and finally with Wellesley (later Duke of Wellington) in Portugal in 1808. He was exonerated from blame for his part in agreeing the Convention of Cintra, the armistice with the French in Portugal, but he never sought another command. He retired with the rank of general and died at Calshot Castle on 18 October 1813. In the 1780s he had taken an active interest in the castle, complaining about its poor

Calshot in 1780 by Paul Sandby. Comparison with the view by the Buck brothers shows the extent of the 1770s alterations, reducing the height of the curtain wall, building the govenor's lodging and alterng the top of the keep to provide a continuous parapet to shield troops armed with muskets (From a private collection)

Calshot in 1792 by Dominic Serres. The strategic setting of the castle, dominating the entrance to Southampton Water, is well shown in this busy scene. A service cutter and a 36-gun frigate are drying their sails, while to the right a merchant ship drifts down on the tide. The unusually high bulwarks running from the mizzen mast to the taffrail on the frigate suggest that the latter may have been adapted for special duty (From a private collection)

state and demanding that repairs and improvements be undertaken. In his last few years he seems to have been content to live there quietly and modestly, in much the same way that his far more distinguished and younger contemporary the Duke of Wellington was later to do at Walmer in Kent.

The coastguards

Well before the end of the Napoleonic Wars Calshot's *raison d'etre* had been substantially diminished; Nelson's victory at Trafalgar and Napoleon's increasing military campaign on mainland Europe had seen to that. For much of the nineteenth century it found a role in the never-ending if less spectacular war against smuggling. The Solent area had long been a favourite haunt of smugglers and for much of the eighteenth-century the revenue cutter *Calshot* had been a familiar if unloved sight on Southampton Water. The sheltered anchorage provided by Calshot Spit was eminently suitable as a place to lie in wait.

After the Napoleonic Wars, Calshot Castle was used as quarters for the coastguards; by 1859 an officer was accommodated in the central tower and married men in the gatehouse. In 1850 and again in 1852 proposals for modernising the castle were considered but nothing was done; it was felt to have only a limited secondary military role.

In 1856 Calshot passed into Admiralty hands when the latter took over the control and running of the coastguard service. For nearly forty more years it continued to serve as accommodation but the development of new weapons and warships was to ensure that its military role was far from over.

The re-arming of the 1890s

In the late 1860s the first effective torpedo was developed by Robert Whitehead. while the 1870s saw European navies experimenting with fast torpedo boats. By the 1880s such craft could reach speeds of 22 knots in sheltered waters and were being built in large numbers by the French navy. The small size and high speed of these new craft made them very difficult targets for existing guns on warships, which could only fire one round every few minutes. The British Admiralty, alarmed, asked gun manufacturers to design and produce a gun able to fire at least twelve aimed rounds a minute. The resultant quick-firing QF weapons were first installed on warships, but by the end of the 1880s torpedo craft had increased in size to the stage where they were sufficiently seaworthy to pose a threat to Britain's coastal shipping, ports and harbours. It was feared that sudden raids by flotillas of such craft - perhaps under cover of darkness - would inflict serious damage to shipping and port installations and be very difficult for the Royal Navy to counter.

On shore, three principal counter-measures were adopted. Coastal forts were provided with QF guns and searchlights and, where appropriate, booms were installed to provide a physical barrier to hostile craft. In the Solent area, effort was concentrated first on modernising the outer forts such as Hurst Castle and the

Needles Battery; the former was equipped with three 12pdr QF guns in 1893. In July 1894 the Admiralty handed over control of Calshot Castle to the War Office for similar weapons to be installed there.

The cramped layout of the Tudor castle was unsuitable for the chosen number of weapons so a separate gun battery was built to the south of the castle. This was begun in September 1895 and completed just over two years later., it mounted two 4.7-inch and four 12prd QF guns commanding the approach to Southampton Water. Nothing now remains of this installation (see page 21).

In the castle itself, the gun embrasures on the northeastern side of the courtyard were adapted for three searchlights, or Defence Electric Lights to use the contemporary term. Their concrete housings still remain. Generators powered by oil engines were installed in the basement of the keep while the two floors above resumed their role as barrack accommodation with eleven men on the first floor and fourteen men on the second. The interior of the gatehouse was extensively altered; the guardroom and its detention cell date from this period as do the cookhouse and storeroom east of the gatehouse. 'Alteration of the old quarters' was begun in September 1890 and completed in November 1896.

Augmenting the battery and searchlights was a boom defence system. The favourable conditions here meant that Southampton Water (with the naval base at Portland, the entrance to Portsmouth Harbour and the Medway at Sheerness) was one of the earliest places in the country to be so protected. The boom was designed to stop surface craft – submarines were not yet considered a serious menace – and initially consisted of a line of hulks (disused ships) which could be secured stem to stern across the navigable channel.

These were linked to 'dolphins', wood and metal towers each armed with two 12-pdr QF guns and a machine gun. The southern end of this boom was immediately to the northeast of the castle. The boom was the responsibility of the Royal Navy which provided four or five elderly gunboats adapted as boom defence vessels. These were normally moored in the River Hamble and were in the charge of a naval commander at Netley. The first boom, which apparently took up to a week to place in position and remove, was replaced by a lighter, purpose-built one in 1909; this was stored on a slipway adjacent to the castle. This boom defence probably remained in active use until the end of the 1914-18 war.

In 1907 Calshot Castle underwent its last major modernisation as a fortress. The keep roof was altered and strengthened to permit the installation of a pair of 12pdr

Bed and soldier's kit in barrack room (see pages 5 and 24)

The boom defence vessels HMS Marina and Reindeer at Devonport, c1904-09. Their sister ship, HMS Melita, was one of six such vessels stationed in Southampton Water by 1910 (National Maritime Museum)

QF guns to augment the adjacent battery. The searchlight generators were removed from the basement which was converted to a cartridge and shell store; a hoist in the centre linked this to the roof. A new generator house, since demolished, was built outside. The 1910 mobilisation plan proposed a wartime complement of 3 officers and 85 other ranks in the castle, with 7 officers and 69 other ranks in private houses and tents to man the castle and the dolphins. Alexandra Hospital, Cosham, was to provide one civilian surgeon and one orderly to take care of the wounded.

Calshot Royal Naval Air Station

Two years later, developments began which were to give Calshot Spit a very different military role during the two world wars. By 1912 aviation had developed to the point where the Admiralty saw a use for planes operating with the fleet in home waters. To do this – aircraft carriers were still in the future – the Admiralty proposed a chain of air stations along the coast from Scapa Flow in the Orkney Islands to Pembroke in west Wales. These were to be sited alongside the sheltered water needed by seaplanes. Calshot was chosen as the most suitable site in Portsmouth Command and on 29 March 1913 Calshot Royal Naval Air Station came into being. Originally there were three wooden sheds for twelve seaplanes; naval personnel were housed in the nearby coastguard cottages and at Warsash, on the north side of Southampton Water.

Calshot Spit from the air. This remarkable photograph was taken in 1917 at one of Calshot's busiest periods as a Royal Naval Air Station. South of the castle are the earthworks of the now vanished gun battery of 1895, and beyond are the hangars and seaplane launching rails. On the foreshore to the left is a twin-hulled flying boat. This was the AD1000, built by J Samuel White of Cowes to mount a 12pdr recoilless cannon for attacking the decks of enemy warships. In 1917 it was the largest seaplane built in this country (Public Record Office)

Twentieth-century Calshot

Until the outbreak of the 1914 war, Calshot air station was used exclusively for experimental purposes; it then became a training base, but by the autumn of 1916 German submarine activity in the Channel was so serious that Calshot mounted regular anti-submarine patrols. Subordinate stations were established at Bembridge on the Isle of Wight and at Portland; these were followed in 1917 by a seaplane base at Newhaven and an airship station at Polegate in Sussex. Before the end of the war, the six-gun battery at Calshot had been stripped of its weapons – perhaps to help overcome the shortage of heavy weapons on the Western Front in France - and the area was used for storing seaplane parts (see page 21). On 1 April 1918, on the abolition of the Royal Naval Air Service, Calshot was transferred to the Royal Air Force and in November 1918 became the School for Naval Co-operation and Aerial Navigation.

In the 1920s and 1930s Calshot continued its experimental and training work, but it was best known as the English base for the famous Schneider Trophy air

Spectators watch Flying Officer Waghorn in a Supermarine Rolls-Royce 6 rounding the turning point off Southsea Castle during his record-breaking flight in the 1929 Schneider Trophy Air Race (Times Newspapers Ltd)

races, started to encourage high-speed flying and finally won outright by Great Britain in 1931. Although the races took place over a course in the Solent, competitors and their seaplanes were housed at Calshot and its keep provided one of the best vantage points for spectators.

In the autumn of 1931 a Seaplane Training Squadron was established at Calshot. When war broke out eight years later, the station's duties were defined as the training of aircrews and repair of seaplanes. In the first winter of the war the only protection against attack was provided by a barge moored next to the castle; on this were two 3-inch anti-aircraft guns and a Bofors (an automatic double-barrelled anti-aircraft gun). The base as a whole was guarded by a detachment of troops from the 8th Hampshire (HD) Regiment, commanded by two acting lieutenants, one the local MP, the other the chairman of the local brewery.

On 24 May 1940, four days before the evacuation from Dunkirk began and when German invasion seemed imminent, the Royal Navy drew up plans to deny the port of Southampton to an invasion force by sinking a line of blockships at the entrance to Southampton Water. These blockships would have been such ships then docked at the port and considered expendable. Fortunately, the crisis passed. Later that year, two 12pdr QF guns were remounted on the roof of the castle and six searchlights were installed. In 1941 these defences were augmented by Bungalow Battery, established opposite on the north shore of Southampton Water and consisting of a further pair of 12pdr QF guns and six searchlights, and by Stone Point Battery some 3 miles southwest of Calshot Castle. Stone Point was equipped with three 6-inch guns on naval mountings; both this and Bungalow

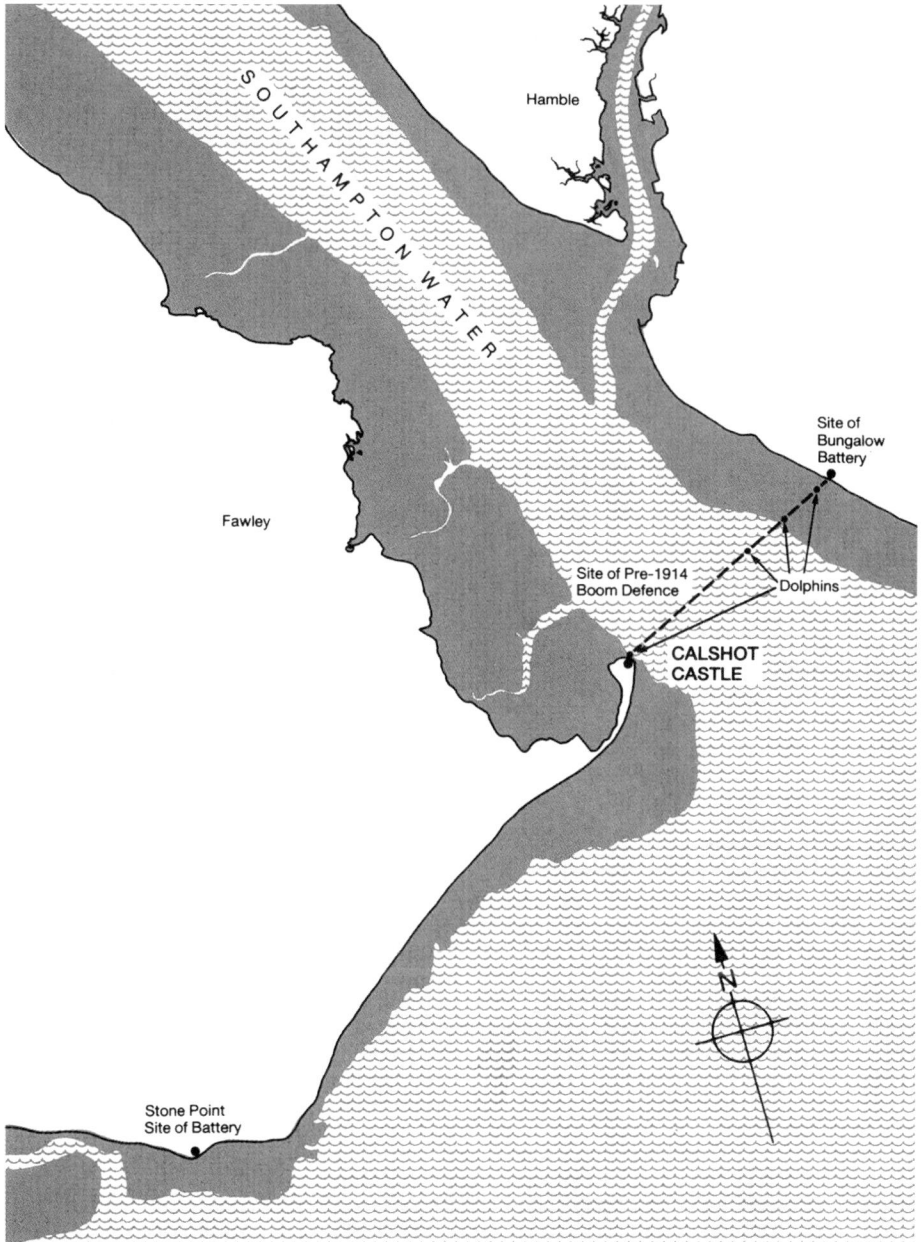

SOUTHAMPTON WATER

Hamble

Site of
Bungalow
Battery

Fawley

Site of Pre-1914
Boom Defence

Dolphins

**CALSHOT
CASTLE**

N

Stone Point
Site of Battery

Late nineteenth- and twentieth-century defences of Southampton Water (Based on Admiralty Chart of 1894)

Nineteenth-century barrack room on the first floor of the keep. Note the beds, part of which slid underneath when not in use so that there was more floor space (see page 5)

Battery formed part of Calshot Fire Command.

Although in the heart of an important air base, Calshot Castle escaped bomb damage; but watchers and guns' crews on its roof were able to see the night skies lit up by the fires of Southampton and Portsmouth after the heavy air raids of 1940 and 1941.

In its time, Henry VIII's castle had fulfilled its task of deterring waterbome attacks on Southampton, but it was largely impotent against this new form of aerial warfare although it has the distinction of being the only Henrician castle to find an active wartime role within an air base.

After the war, advances in aviation gradually made the great flying boats obsolete and with them bases such as Calshot. In 1953 the station was transferred to Maintenance Command, becoming 238 Maintenance Unit before it was finally closed.

The castle itself, stripped of its wartime armaments, reverted to its nineteenth-century role and once again provided accommodation for coastguards. On completion of their new tower, the coastguards left the castle which has been restored by English Heritage to its pre-1914 appearance. Around it, the former hangars of RAF Calshot have a new use as an activity centre run by the county council.